HUMANS
and other
ANIMALS

HUMANS
and other
ANIMALS

A Collection of Fifty
Man-Beast Poem/Stories
Paul Edward Gainor

© 2017 by Paul Edward Gainor

All rights reserved. No part of this publication may be reproduced, distributed or transmitted in any form or by any means, without prior written permission, except in the case of brief quotations embodied in critical articles or reviews.

Green Bananas Publishing
P.O. Box 661
Fennville, MI 49408
www.pgwriter876@gmail.com

Publisher's Note: This is a work of fiction. Names, characters, places, and incidents are a product of the author's imagination. Locales and public names are sometimes used for atmospheric purposes. Any resemblance to actual people, living or dead, or to businesses, companies, events, institutions, or locales is completely coincidental.

ISBN Paperback: 978-0-9994766-8-0
ISBN eBook: 978-0-9994766-9-7

Book Cover and Interior Design: Ghislain Viau

To Gess, without whom this book, indeed this life, would not be possible.

Contents

Introduction	1
A Glance	3
Acolytes	9
Another Dream	10
Ant	13
A Big Black Dog	14
Badger	15
Bear	19
Conversation with a Cuiza	23
Dialogue with my Father	26
Diana, My Girl	29
Eclipse	31
Fawn	32
Few Squirrels	33
Fiona, Awake!	34
Flies	36
Fly	37
Frost	38
Gate Opening	41
Golandrina Truce	42
I Died for You	47
I Have to Dwell	48
I Lost You	49
Insufferably Bright	51

La Via Contraria	52
Mira Ballena!	54
Mouse	55
Phyllis: Thanks for the Light	57
Piper	58
Rabbit in a Cage	61
Poetic Time Warp	65
Coming up a Rarie	66
Rhythm & Rhyme	69
Robin	71
Spooky Wedding	72
The Smartest Man	73
Squirrels and Thanksgiving	76
Stoning Dogs	78
Tepid Revenge	86
The Flock	88
(Under) The Porch	90
The Doing of a Thing	95
The Glass	96
To Marry?	98
Too Sensitive	99
Turkeys	101
Two Burros	104
Weather Backcast	106
What Exactly	107
When I Was a Child	109
Yet I Am	112
You Tried and Failed	113
Acknowledgments	117
Author's Biography	119

"We are part of the earth and it is part of us. The perfumes flowers are our sisters; the deer, the horse, the great eagle: these are our brothers. All things are connected like the blood which unites one's family."

—Chief Seattle, Suquamish Tribe, 1786-1866

"Unraveling the mysteries of DNA has provided eye-opening confirmation that we share infinitely more with animals than most of us ever imagined."—Canadian Geographic magazine, December 2009

Introduction

This book, beginning with its title, deliberately blurs the distinction between human and "other" animals.

I didn't set out to write a book half about animals. I didn't discover them; they discovered me. They wandered onto my stage in the middle of the play, revealing often-curious, near-human behaviors that I couldn't have invented. Then they stole scenes and leading roles from the human actors around them, charming me and, I hope, you—the reader.

Animal characters include a cheeky *cuiza* (a Mexican lizard), a jaunty sandpiper, a caged rabbit in love with his captor, a charming dog-thief, a carefree pair of runaway burros, a valiant Doberman Pinscher, a family of breaching Humpback Whales, Mexican swallows bent on occupying the author's home, and a line of parading wild American turkeys.

The human side of this collection carries us from the simplicity of children observing adult secret behaviors from their hiding place under a porch, to the close-encounter between a revered poet laureate and a student poet-to-be, a terrified Mexican boy being menaced by a pack of dogs, a pampered *senora* flaunting her wealth in touristy Puerto Vallarta, Mexico, a *Gringo* who knew too much for his own good, and a shocking image of imminent death in a bathroom mirror.

These tales approach life in both human animal and non-human animal terms. They are meant to be shared, read aloud and enjoyed for their musicality, meter and rhyme, humor, life lessons, and the adventures they relate.

A Glance

Bent over I was, trowel in hand,
Intense in my concentration
Tending my country garden,
When I felt an odd sensation,

It wasn't a bee, for it was too strong;
It wasn't a bird—too far from a tree;
It wasn't a leaf; it lasted too long—
Nor was it a breeze, it seemed to me;

It jarred the foggy solitude that
Had hovered over me for days;
It broke the eerie still I felt,
Forestopped my turbid gaze.

There came a country woodsman
So close upon my face
His jacket touched my collar
As I dug aside a trace.

I didn't see him passing,
So fast he came and went;
I barely glimpsed his ruddy beard,
His rough complexion's tint.

He called so cheerily to me,
Tossed back his head to look,
I caught his sturdy aspect
As manly strides he took.

I craned my neck to see him;
I struggled to my feet,
But he was gone, a vision lost,
A man I'd never meet.

I looked beyond the land-rise
That led to the ravine;
He disappeared into it;
No more could he be seen.

The memory of him lingers,
Though just a glance I saw,
His face, his smile, his swagger,
The jutting of his jaw.

Humans and Other Animals

I couldn't help but notice though,
As he waved his gloveless hand—
His sturdy fingers, long and strong—
There was no wedding band.

Much one can tell, I reckon,
Though just a glance I caught,
About the mettle of a man,
His work, how he is wrought—

In body as well as mind, of course;
The turn of the wrist, you see,
May dismiss or may invite—
Who knows which it will be?

The palm reveals the hours
He labors to provide
For table, home, and housewife,
Should there be one (Or she died).

Let's say she may be dead and gone
And left to him at home
A hearth, a house and many a child,
A bed, so cold, so lone.

Or if his palm be soft and white,
Spared toil for he lives single,
He may be shy and quiet,
Averse to mix and mingle.

And his cap, one can tell
Much from its style, color and shape,
For his was a tuque held up by curls
So handsomely on the nape

Of his neck thick and tan;
No one could mistake him—a man
Of sound habits—for one loose and fey;
In weighty matters; sure no one can.

Attire not to be ignored,
His britches were of leather
Cinched tight at the waist, close at the hip,
Legs snug against the weather.

His shirt, as best I saw it,
Was ample at the shoulder
Tucked neat into his waist-band;
Back, hips even bolder.

His turning, though, showed me
Cheeks of such roundness,
I could not help but see
Their strength, their manly soundness.

His feet were covered crudely,
Though shod he needed be,
To tread across the forest
With boots up to the knee.

I barely saw his visage
As he shot to me a wink,
His eyes all brown and sparkling,
His lips all thick and pink.

His teeth gleamed in the sunlight,
So broadly shone his smile
I scarcely could have missed it
Way off beyond a mile;

A ruddy, rough complexion
Was brown from sun-seared days
In woodlots and in meadows
In search of daily prey;

His trusty ax hung grandly
From rope-cinched leather trousers—
He used to cut from Birches
Switches, whips or dowsers.

Not much do I remember
Of this man of the forest:
Voice, looks or his appearance—
My memory's the poorest.

I had no time to frame his face
Nor body in my mind
Except to know should he return
I'd grab his sleeve next time.

Should soon a woodsman happen
To brush against your collar,
Remember my sad lesson:
Don't wait until he passes:
Holler!

La Cruz de Huanacaxtle, Mexico
February 13, 2015

Acolytes

They trail the shepherd's languid pace,
Obey each footfall, turn, and nod;
First come the doleful acolytes,
Imperfect in line, reflecting his place.

Then come the feisty rebel crew,
A dog ahoof should they disobey.

Finally follow the placid sheep,
Ruminants who can't recall
Why they'd ever thought to stray.

Another Dream/Outside of Time

Another night, another dream
Your body twisted, tortured, shaking.
I know your movements tell of strife,
A life beyond our bedstead, quaking.

Events afar yet in your mind
Call out from dreams and so I waken;
I listen keenly for a sign
Of why your sleep has been so shaken.

And then I hear an eerie call,
An oblong word, you cry my name:
You call to me, "Paaauull,"
Like bubbles from a circle frame.

And when I reach to take your hand;
"Respond to me," you then exclaim.
"I'm here my darling," I call back
Across the void from wake to dream.

When you awake I say, "You dreamt;
You called my name from in your dream."
"Inside a building, we were locked,
Could not escape, or so it seemed.

"As headlights from a car passed by
I crossed the room to windows where
We'd hoped to make escape, but then
A grate was closed upon us there.

"And then, you're blinded by the light,
No sign of me, no window, door.
Absent in the darkening night,
You couldn't see me anymore.

"And then across the gap you called
From terror of the dream to bed;"
The span from dream to waking crossed,
I pressed your hand and then I said:

"My darling, it's a dream; I'm here."
I pondered, wondering did you hear
Inside the dream or from awake;
Were you in there and I out here?

Did you awake and come to me,
Or did I arrive to join your dream?
An instant's reach across the pale
Connected us, as on a beam.

If I could join your dream this way,
And you could take my eager hand,
Might we yet cross another void
From death to life and back again?

We'll wait, my darling, for the day
When one is here and one away
To test the death-and-earth divide;
Rejoin on death's first holiday.

AnotherDreamPoem020716

Ant

An ant I saw atop my backyard pool,
Swimming, desperate to stay alive,
Spindly legs stroking haplessly,
Wanting only that second to survive.

Nature never meant him to swim,
Provided him no defense to drowning.
He struggled for the edge to find a brim,
He twitched as I watched, frowning.

What use can be this bug to nature's kind,
For what good in life had it prepared him?
But then compassion seized my torpid mind;
Since life connects us all as creatures—Spare him!

And with a flick I scooped him in my hand;
He landed softly on the nearby ground;
And in that momentary flash of time
Our beings crossed, that second interbound.

A Big Black Dog

A big black dog
Follows me home,
His murky aspect
Not his alone,

But mine from youth.
I know you well;
Come in and sit.
Tales you could tell

Of early tortures,
For you were my pet,
A doleful witness
To spitefulness.

121913

Badger

A Badger came out front one noon.
A fine young fellow was he!
And when he heard my slightest noise
He fled with all celerity.

He scampered smartly to the woods,
Though not designed for speed or grace,
Not wishing confrontation
With any of the human race.

I was mistaken on sight of him,
Witness the mounds of sandy loam—
Raised tunnels I thought were his—
I took for tubes he made his home.

I took him for a Groundhog
—A Woodchuck, some might say;
But a Woodchuck would've found a hole
To make his get-away.

I should've known he was too large,
His stride too short and awkward,
To flee into a narrow hole;
For him to fit would be absurd.

Instead he merely ran from me,
A dory through a sea of grass,
Pale pelt of his broad back propelled—
Graceless—as fast as he could pass.

His cumbersome construction
Not meant to sprint or race,
Still made impressive time
Vacating his feeding base.

What a surprise when he returned!
The second time he stood upright,
Balanced steady on his rear paws,
Surveying all in sight.

He showed me then his handsome face—
A dark mask shadowed it by half—
His eyes gleamed as he looked around;
He dove for grubs behind tall grass.

Humans and Other Animals

At this event he didn't spy me,
Quiet at my home's front door;
I was in awe of his grandeur—
My regal returned visitor.

In such a standing attitude
His piercing eyes surveyed
The lawn for nearby predators,
Yet he was wholly undismayed.

He dove and clawed till he unearthed
The luscious grubs beneath the grass;
While I enjoyed his badger-show,
He feasted ceaseless, unabashed.

O badger, badger, what a sight,
To witness such a creature,
In his native habitat!
What a spectacle of nature!

From north Pacific waters
To the bluffs of Michigan—
This is where your breed was born;
This is where your life began.

Are you a boar or a sow?
I don't know—how does one tell?
To know you'd need to be a Badger;
Spring's events may yet foretell.

Badgers rarely socialize
Except in breeding season,
And then a springtime's batch of kits
May tumble from their mother's den.

Will you bring a mate to show,
To grace my April lea?
Will my front lawn next spring become
Host to your family?

BadgerPoem092116

Bear

Across the road a blur of fur
Dashed past from wood to wood.
Why it ran I wasn't sure,
Far out front my auto's hood.

Bear! There could be no doubt.
Its back was humped, its buttocks tucked,
Uncoiling robust energy
Toward a thicket wherein it ducked.

Front legs outstretched to full extended,
It grabbed each inch of asphalt crossed,
Fleeing, panicked till pavement ended;
Its normal confidence was lost.

Each spring the yearling cubs—dismissed
By sows reclaiming dens for home—
Are forced to sectors that weren't meant
For youngsters such as they to roam.

A hundred yards before my car
I viewed its hasty rout;
From thicket west to thicket east—
Bear silhouette, there was no doubt.

South Michigan is not the normal
Home to Black Bears seen "Up North."
This one was frightened, panic-stricken
To leave its lair and sally forth.

They're pushing south from Holland now,
To Indiana's shore
Of Michigan's lake sandy-brow.
They share our home, they're rare no more.

Ursus Americanus:
"With black or extremely brown fur,
Covers twenty miles per day"—
(No wonder they're not where they were.)

"Solitary animal;
"Except when it's breeding;
"Will eat whatever it can get;
"Opportunistic in feeding."

Humans and Other Animals

We mustn't get too friendly though,
For if we do we're dangerous
To man's and bear's posterity;
The bear will usually lose.

"Eats anything from ants to bees,
"Including carrion;
"Indulges its taste for berries;
"Has hunted newborn fawn."

Now you're part of the local fauna—
Along with turkeys, fox and rabbits –
But you require special care;
We must now yield, forebear your habits.

Black Bears? They bring something new;
Feared and fearsome fearless beasts—
We don't expect them in our gardens,
Nor at our doors nor window-seats;

Nor on our rural, country lawns
When in the morn we open drapes
In our homes at early dawn
As startled fawns make their escapes.

Bears: not winsome,
But fearsome;
Not graceful—power-full,
Not beautiful, but awe-some.

Sure you'll flee from confronting me
Before I see you, O bear.
We'll see you when to tree you bring
A fuzzy cub and then a pair.

Revered by local Indians,
Hunted out by wary settlers,
You're back, these many decades past,
You're welcomed, all together.

It's now we share your habitat,
Of meadows, hills and woods.
Come back, Black Bear, our long-gone friend;
This time you've found a home for good.

August 8, 2016

Conversation with a Cuiza

Awakened by a cuiza,
I twisted to my rear
To hear the tiny fellow
Chuck-chucking in my ear.

I was in my *hamaca*;
He nearly touched my arm;
"You swung so close to me," he said,
"I had to raise alarm.

"I am so small a weakling
And you so big and strong
I felt a need, I had to speak;
I couldn't wait too long,

"For fear your swinging hammock
Might crush me to the wall
And sure a cuiza small as I
Would die from such a fall."

"It's true," I said, "a cuiza's soft,
With flesh no more than jelly—
Pale green, transparent lizard
And tender in the belly.

"You're given feet with suckers
That hold you low or high,
Upside-down and sideways,
To help you catch a fly.

"Your bones are soft and pliant
Your tail is long and narrow;
Sit patient for an hour,
Dart forward like an arrow."

Said he: "When I awoke you,
You moved your arm just so;
I hastened toward the ceiling
And gobbled up a row

"Of unsuspecting termites
Crawling on a beam;
They were to be my dinner,
And you to miss a dream."

Humans and Other Animals

"I lost a dream," I said to him,
"When you awakened me,
From afternoon *siesta*,
Foreshortened as you see.

"At night you come a chucking,
In tones so loud and clear,
Calling to your lost mate
For all at home to hear.

"Your laughter seldom roists me
But now it had such power,
Your chucking-call surprised me
At such an early hour."

And then the tiny creature
From up the ceiling high
Chuck-chucked again down to me
While saying his good-bye.

La Cruz de Huanacaxtle, Mexico
January 2015

Dialogue with my Father on the Centennial Of His Birth

"What do you have to say to me,
In this your hundredth year?
What of import must you tell
You couldn't say when you were here?"

"'I love you, son,'" might you not say?
"'I'm proud to know you. How've you been?
Remember me; let's reminisce
On things we didn't dare back when.'

"What would you say to me, my Dad?
We left so much unsaid back then.
How man-to-man-austere you were—
A man who never loved a man.

"We dared not touch as man and boy,
Though I yearned for your strong hand;
I felt unloved, untouchable;
Fatherless, without a man.

"You'd lay your hand on my forehead
To see if I was ailing.
I'd wished your calloused hand would stay;
Your touch could bring me healing."

"How can it be, my son, my son?
I've longed to tell you to your face,
What I'd admired you'd become—
A man I wanted to embrace."

"You say, my Dad, you wanted what?—
To hold me in your arms, declare
In sixty years you failed to hold
A son you'd loved but didn't dare?"

"Now I can tell the truth, my son—
How much I ached to hold you near;
To tell you how I cared for you,
To let you know it wasn't queer

"For me to cherish you and say,
'You know my love can never die;
You know you're precious to me, son;
I'm proud to be your dad today,

"'And ever-more when life is done.'"
"What did you say, my loving Dad?
That you love me as much as I ... –
A century of love we've had?"

"What's that you say, my son? How so?
You're now beyond my sixty years?
Your hair is whiter than mine then,
You've passed my age by twelve full years?"

"Yes Dad, it's true; as decades passed
I have become your elder;
Yet still I am your self-same son,
And you are still my father.

"But wait, my father-Dad of Love,
Of what were we then so ashamed?
For gender's sake was warmth suppressed,
And for this both of us are blamed?"

"Love of a man and love of men
Hew differently applied to sons.
It took these years for us to learn,
We've always had the love we've won."

Lloyd Clement Gainor was born August 24, 1916, died April 25. 1978.

September 18, 2016

Diana My Girl

A man came after me and my dog,
"I'll kill that dog," he said, raising a stick
Above his head, steady
Ready to flog
The head of my Diana,
A valiant Doberman.

She could have taken him out
With only a leap,
Pinned him helpless to the dusty road;
Instead I held her fast upon her leash
She didn't creep.

"Touch my dog and you're a dead man," I said;
"She knows commands
And you can bet she'll mind."

I knew the guy as Fred, a neighbor,
A man so full of hate he liked to brag
Of his acumen in strong-man shows—
Victories to prove he was no fag.

A little guy, a full-foot short of me,
A Napoleonic specimen indeed,
Perhaps he had to prove himself
Superior in strength, valor or deed.

It wasn't our first engagement, you see,
For Fred had a lot to prove
—and maybe his enragement
Provided angry fuel to help him move.

Talk was that Fred beat his stepson,
And cuffed and clipped his comely wife, Lee Ann—
No surprise both blonder, taller than he,
And to himself Fred proved he was a man.

La Cruz de Huanacaxtle, Mexico

Eclipse

Today at six there was a lunar eclipse.
I lay in bed; I caught it on the news,
Full round its moonlight flooded my ellipse;
Purple clouds between obscured my views,
Then opened to reveal a partial orb,
A bloody ochre then to reabsorb.

June 15, 2016

Fawn

One day at dawn
I spied a spotted fawn
Nibbling grass on my front lawn;
I turned and it was gone.

                Ganges, Michigan October 12, 2016

Few Squirrels

Pondering my move from city to country,
I sit sipping coffee beneath a Magnolia tree
Laden with blooms of white, mauve, and lavender.
A Cardinal twitters and flits among its rooms

As he regales me, ignoring the squirrel
That climbs below and grooms a furry cheek,
A fuzzy tail. I sit, sipping, watching
Friends I'll lose in moving so far away.

Why are there so few squirrels and birds
Around our home in the country?

Detroit, Michigan 2013

Fiona, Awake!

At break of dawn you sigh as if to say,
"A lovely evening we had yesterday."

And then a high-pitched yawn you emit;
From my bedside you nuzzle my arm pit.

I can't miss the urgency of your cries,
The passionate rhythm of your deepening sighs.

Like a tambor you beat an insistent tattoo.
"It's day, so what are we going to do?"

Why the raucous flapping of your ears?
And why the persistent drumming on my bed
With your tail to raise the holy dead?
"I want out," you say. "Can't you hear?"

With that last straw reluctantly I arise
And you follow me eagerly to the door.
Another day, another dog-surprise;
As neighbors offer you a bone—and more.

My hobo girl, my frequent nighttime guest,
Now that you've enjoyed your food and rest,
Off you go to beg another meal,
To win a treat, another heart to steal.

February 22, 2016,
La Cruz de Huanacaxtle, Mexico

Flies

For what purpose exists the fly?
The fly a human can never please,
For when it touches food it brings disease.

"But what about the maggot?" you ask.
"Does it not precede the fly?
And bring with it a kit of tools
To scavenge moist carrion dry?"

Squirming and turning in garbage rot
Or the corpse of a cat, rat or mouse,
The white of the wriggling maggot
Brings order to Nature's house.

Fly!

Mountain Ash all filigreed
Pale green against a sky
So clear in azure firmament
Invites the Grackle: Fly!

Frost*

We met when we were men—you
venerable, ending your career—
And I was young, a naif.

You didn't notice me,
But not a move of yours
Escaped my scrutiny.

Your voice and hands shook with age;
You clenched the lectern with farmer's paws
Your papers famously aflutter.

We sang your noble anthem starchly—
A poem with music for the occasion—
To revere your work, your life, in awe.

---

* A recollection of what is believed to have been Robert Frost's final public appearance, at the field house of the University of Detroit November 4, 1962. Frost's *The Gift Outright* was put to music by Don Large, director of the University of Detroit Chorus, and that day was performed by the chorus, of which the author was a student member. Frost died at age eighty-eight on January 29, 1963.

Humans and Other Animals

Your hair arose like stalks of wheat
Above your ruddy Yankee
Farmer's sun-flecked face.

You faltered at first, then commenced the voice:
You were too old to be liberal
Too conservative to be young.

Grateful you still had life to speak,
We could not fault your politics;
You passed weeks later.

All we heard was the rhythm,
The rhyme of your words;
Your wisdom fell deaf on youthful ears.

Now old like you, I wonder how
You captured the lamb, the wind,
The land and their nature.

You could have been my plainsman
Grandfather,
Were you Midwestern

And had his pen cut
As keenly as his Iowa
Sod-buster's plow.

December 19, 2013

Gate Opening

The sound my gate announces when you've gone
A squeak, a clang, it makes a certain groan
That causes wonder: Why it sits unopened
For all the time it's guarded me alone.

Open then, then closed and ever since,
It blocks a path that passes either way,
A path that one may take while I await
Blossoms, breath, a homecoming bouquet.

Should I be here when you return one day,
I'll be rewarded by the groan, the squeak;
It is for your welcome smile I stay.
And well-oiled gates forsake the joy they'd speak.

June 10, 2016

Golondrina Truce

In Spring the Golondrinos prepare their nests,
An impressive feat of engineering,
Beaksful of mud brought to their covered rests,
Perfect bowls for tiny swallow-rearing.

Yellow-breasted and blue coat-tailed men
Flap furious, scream ear-jarring cries
To tempt the plain and pale and wrenish hen
To join a hopeful egg-raising enterprise.

Up until this point all's well with me—
They swallow mosquitoes and that's to the good,
Except they want their business place to be
Abreast our ceiling beams' protected wood.

We watch, amazed to see their fervid zeal.
They flit, they flash, they dash, they swoop; they poop!
What's a little poop? No big deal—
But now we've got the entire flocking group.

Humans and Other Animals

After warnings, they dart toward the ceiling,
Making *us* feel unwelcome in *their* space.
By now I'm off-balance, and I'm reeling;
Then I have a bird fly in my face.

Now, of course, stuff happens:
Excremental bombs fly from mid-air,
Splattering walls with carbon-colored droppings;
Painting Dali-esque patterns everywhere.

Oh yes, and they're dive-bombing all the while,
Defending their precious nests from our attack,
Matching wits against our human guile,
Moving in and never looking back.

It's them or us; either they leave or we must!
They were here first, you say, and you're right;
But we built this house from timbers and dust;
We won't be leaving soon; we'll stay and fight.

Battle joined, our house is no Capistrano;
Birds, eggs, nests and all must depart—
Or our home is a magnet for swallow guano;
We'll get aggressive, but how and where do we start?

Brooms, mops and sticks are brought into battle—
Anti-aircraft—the best we could muster.
A can full of marbles makes a fearful rattle;
We're Sitting Bull and they Colonel Custer!

A plague attacks by northwest in hordes—
No kinder than what Moses sent Pharaoh.
We're out-numbered, outgunned, on the boards;
They have the air; our choices now are narrow.

Banzai and bombs away! Swallows: Six,
People: Zero; Ack-Ack up! Fire!
It's *South Pacific* without the music,
Battle conditions are becoming dire.

Down they dive, precision-flying;
Onto the open porch they dodge and dance;
Defenses are few, though we are trying.
Counter-offensive? We've a less-than-even chance.

Valiant hen stalls half-way to the nest.
Ack-Ack engaged—a broom comes after,
Delivers targeted shots to the breast,
Whacks that hapless hen to Forever-After.

Humans and Other Animals

We lay her down for the rest of the flock to view;
Showing we humans aren't to be trifled with;
Here's what you can expect, the rest of you,
Your own *Lullaby-to-Birdland* death.

But oh, then I examined
Her: Pale breast, lovely forking tail,
Yellow beak and perfectly-formed head;
My triumph crumbled, my victory withered, paled.

How could I have killed this fearless little mite?
She only wanted to propagate her breed;
I'd won the day, but lost the moral right,
I'd failed in human heart, failed indeed.

We scrape the muddy nests from off the walls;
Poison them with chemical deterrent;
Stretch nets across the house's gates and halls,
Assurred the pesky birds won't be recurrent.

The battle with the Golondrinas won,
We relish our newfound freedom from the hen,
Till another pair of Golondrinas come,
Nesting outside our covered porch again.

Now they chit-chit-chatter if we come too near,
Remind us of their need for flight and nest;
Now on our porch we hold our swallows dear,
A truce is won. An armistice is best!

March 30, 2015 La Cruz de Huanacaxtle, Mexico

I Died for You

I died for you a thousand times;
I died for you just once.

The thousand were the times in life
I pined for you without response.

The once was far more wounding
You left without farewell;

The once such pain and anguish brought
No thought could grief dispel.

I Have to Dwell

I have to dwell on what I've done,
Not dream of deeds forgot.
For sure I'll gain much more this way;
Regrets all count for naught.

I Lost You

In the night you woke to cry: "I lost you!"
I knew it was a dream for I was there.
At dawn's first light I asked: "Please tell me true,
What came into your quiet sleeping, dear?"

You gasped to me: "A frightening place …
You went ahead without me to explore …
Every circumstance of time and space,
While you left me behind, sore

"In my misery that you were gone—
I know not how or why or wherefore—
I feared injury or death would be done
And I'd be unable to restore

"You to health, life, to bring you back."
"But you know," I said, "I couldn't fail to find you,
To you somehow for sure I'd find a track;
Is your faith in me so weak that you'd believe

That I could leave your side so easily?"
"No," you said, "except if you were dead,
For then you'd lack control and I'd
Fall behind with you so far ahead

"That you'd be lost to me in our next life."
"But then, my love, I would reach back to pull
You through the membrane of Death which separates
Worlds that ghostly spirits cross at will."

"But what if spirits blocked my way back in?"
"Your doubt reveals to me how poor a faith
Inhabits love's powerful command:
'Arise, and greet my waiting spirit's wraith.'"

February 20, 2016
La Cruz de Huanacaxtle, Mexico

Insufferably Bright

Why so insufferably bright and cheerful
In a world so dark and fearful,
When our race is soon to crash
In heaps of hateful, smoldering ash?

At end of day we pray forget
Each flaw of character, regret;
Pass from this life through Death's dark knell
In near escape of mankind's future Hell.

July 20, 2016

La Via Contraria

Driving down a narrow street in Old Town
Puerto Vallarta, Mexico, I came
Nose-to-nose with a *senora*, a frown
On her lovely face as if to blame

Me, as I raised my hands in query
On how I was to pass her vehicle,
Which blocked my auto's way so clearly
That you couldn't pass a nickel

Or a flattened peso between our cars.
Now, this was a cobbled path built
For donkey carts and *senoras* with jars
Upon their heads packed to the hilt

With crafts made at home and brought to market
In the days when the Yankee dollar
Fetched twenty pesos however you marked it;
Mexicans were short, we taller.

But now, now I'm here and in the right,
My quizzical smile will surely clear this up.
For I turned rightly at the corner light;
All she need do now is back up.

Something in her calm demeanor
Might have warned the cocky *Gringo* in me,
But I didn't catch it; between her
Unfazed glance and pulling up so nimbly:

"Senor, es la via contraria!"
Oh my God, I muttered, my righteous frown
Failing like an off-key aria;
It's a one-way street I'm going down!

A head-slap and a humbled flourish—
I felt an ass, a *burro* with saddle-bags
On the street, like old times. Amateurish,
I reversed my Chevy over cobbles and crags.

Sweetly smiling, her hauteur was incontrovertible
For all to see how high up she was bred.
As I backed away from her plush new convertible,
I nodded *adios* to *burros*, saddlebags and native ladies
    with jars upon their heads.

December 12, 2015

Mira, Ballena!

A blinding flash of black
Then a crack of sound.
A puff of vaporous white,
A splash of eerie height
And then a tail, upbound.
A crash, a slash of light.

A whale!
    A cow.
        A male.
            Follows then the elfin calf.

Ponderous monsters of the Deep.
Creatures race unseen below,
Gain speed to break the Blue above,
To raise their elephantine prows,
Depart the murkish leagues of deep nightmarish waters,
    And rend the brilliant sky in half.

February 15, 2002,
La Cruz de Huanacaxtle, Nayarit, Mexico

Mouse

I heave a mouse of pink and white
Off the deck to the ravine:
Rest in peace, my deceased friend,
Intruder of my basement scene.

How the colors of your sleek
And lovely carcass echo Spring-
Time's hues you now rejoin.
Shall we list the tunes they sing?

The color of your rosebud nose
The purple of the Lilac shows.

Hues of your tiny nimble paw
Pink blooms of Wisteria draw.

Fur on your fair, plump tummy
Blooms of Apple bring to me.

And your furry mouse-face hints
At blossoms bursting Nature's tints—
Coloration shown to me
In your dustpan destiny.

As your corpus sails through air
Rodent hues rhyme everywhere.

Adios, my furry friend,
From Nature's palette and back again.

June 15, 2016

Phyllis: Thanks for the Light

Won't you come and sit a while?
Bring the twinklings of your smile
For your lucid countenance
Showers us with innocence
And your sparkles of delight
Pierce with beams the darkest night.

To Phyllis Steiner, Bucerias, Mexico,
December 2013

Piper

A flock of Pipers in the sand
Drew me to walk among them to see
If any would stay and
One did; he surprised me.

As the others whorled and whirled
In a cyclone of feathers and wings,
The tiny cock who stayed now twirled
And strangely strutted a Highland Fling

Mysteriously at my feet,
Then picked up a tiny twig
And held it just so; and beat
A tattoo and danced an Irish Jig.

Then feathers aflutter, he moved
So gingerly, I was transfixed
To see a Piper that proved
So facile at such tricks

Humans and Other Animals

As to amuse and amaze
A beach-walker such as I;
Then I moved closer, but he was unfazed
And chirped and twittered as if to fly;
But instead of surmounting the dusty beach
His gyrating wings halted abruptly cold;
Then he darted and gamboled just out of reach,
Tossed his stick into the air and caught it so bold

His form a drum major
Could hardly surpass;
He twirled the stick with such grace you'd wager
The fellow graduated at the top of his class.

I glanced down the beach to see
If nearby came a witness
To confirm my sanity,
To show I'm no vapid, witless

Imaginer of improbable delusion
And that this dancing bird
Was not just an illusion
That had dreamily occurred.

Then suddenly rang an alarm,
Disrupting the still of the day;
And evading witness, exuding charm,
My secret friend then flitted away.

February 6, 2015;
La Cruz de Huanacaxtle, Mexico

A Rabbit in a Cage

I am a rabbit
In a cage.
My farmer's here,
Won't let me out
To eat the luscious
Lettuce I see
In my yard.

It's mine but it's not.
I can see and smell it
But not taste it.

I want the carrots
And the parsley,
Beans, and celery;
But what is there
For me?
Pellets.

All year long
I wait to see
When my farmer
Will open my pen.

In the Spring
I anticipate
The taste of
Each leaf,
Each root
Each beet,
Each bean.

But I can't
Open the gate.
Only he can,
So I wait.

My offense
Is a mystery
To me.

Humans and Other Animals

The reason
For my captivity
I cannot see.
What have I done
To be held here
With him there,
Where I can see
But can't reach
What he grows for me.

So I wait.

How I love my farmer.
All I want
And need he has.
I spy it
Through my wires,
And desire it
So earnestly
While I nibble
My pellets
To sustain life;
But it's not living
—anyway not what I
Would call
Living.

I am sad
For the humans I see
Outside my cage—
Are they free?
They never get
To the lettuce they want,
But they live—
If living it is—
On squares of leaves
While the greens
Of beans and lettuce
And beets
Wither outside
Their pens.

So they eat only
What their farmer puts
Into their bowls.

Would you open
their cages
If you could?

I would.

Detroit, Michigan, May 17, 2011

Poetic Time Warp

A man out of his own time,
I can't surrender meter;
I won't relinquish rhyme.

Frost it was who said it best:
Free verse is tennis without a net.

Coming Up a Rarie

I'm a Rarie; are you one too?
I learned it early, way before school.

People read it on my face;
I tried to hide it to avoid disgrace.

A Rarie's a weird thing,
Not normal at all.

We hide in our closets;
We sneak down the hall.

Sometimes we play with dolls,
Not trucks and cars, the usual toys,
And may be better at Hop-Scotch
And play more with girls than boys.

In high school I tried out for tennis,
But that was a Rarie thing, too,
So I toughed my way up to football,
As a Rarie sometimes will do.

Humans and Other Animals

I had to learn to tackle and block
And which to do when,
But I was blocking when I should tackle,
Confused third down with first and ten.

The rules of basketball, I found,
A Rarie like me could better grasp;
A round ball in a round hole
I picked up on fast.

But a Rarie I was while
Out on the floor;
I tried to fit in,
But felt different the more;

Till college—I majored in Theatre Arts—
I paralyzed audiences
In mirthful responses
To my most serious parts.

My minor was English (Lit.
of course)
And finally the Rarie found his place
—I had no remorse.

I started with Shakespeare,
Moved on to Dickinson and Frost,
Tried my hand at short stories,
Strove hard at all cost.

I created, I wrote in rhythm and rhyme;
An English sonnet I could carry;
What's my place now?
I'm a Liter-Rarie!

February 21, 2015,
La Cruz de Huanacaxtle, Mexico

Rhythm & Rhymes

All the time rhythms and rhymes sail through my mind;
I can't stop them;
Though my voice be still as a mime's
And be I in York or Bethlehem

That rhyming thing declines to cease,
Beyond all reason will not abate,
Stubborn against quiet or peace,
How does a poet evade this fate?

And counting always beats per line,
The rhythmic pattern makes me drum
Till every line is fit and fine,
And each attains the self-same sum.

Were I more like e.e. cummings
And less like Edna St. Vincent Millay,
Would I hew less to what such drummings,
Soundings, ringings, parsings convey?

Dickinson's feathered thing in the soul,
Frost with promises to keep,
Ravens haunting Edgar Allen Poe,
So poorly do these lines compete!

Robin

From meadow to ravine a Robin glides,
Yet always trees herself abreast
My perch, tree astride
The deck from where I glimpse her breast.
A flash of orange swoops about her wings
Aflutter with such urgency I wonder
What draws this creature? Could be anything.

Could she be hunting bugs or berries?
But no, the season and species aren't right
To yield what the ambitious mother carries
Home to nest from the tree she alights.

It's too late for Robin chicks in Michigan,
By now her young must surely be a-wing.
I creep to glimpse her tree to see again.
Might I be wrong about such a curious thing?
Does she hide a secret in a place
Too low to earth to shelter hatchling chicks?
Yet there at level to my face I'm shocked:
What? Nesting chicks ignoring nature's tricks!

Ganges, Michigan 2014

Spooky Wedding
(To Ron & Chuck)

They were married on Halloween,
Flaming faggots and pitchforks were seen;
All went without a hitch,
Vows spoke without a twitch,
But who was the warlock
And which one was the witch?

October 31, 2014

The Smartest Man

I always wished I could collect
The praise of friends for intellect,
But rarely do I realize success.

Just yesterday I met a man
Whose observations always ran
To certainty, but never to a guess.

Admire him, I said to me,
There's much to learn from one as he
Whose reading must exceed my paltry list.

Weighty authors, alive and dead,
In French he certainly has read,
Capturing each phrase's lilt and gist.

In Spain they use a different word,
He said to make me look absurd,
(though I was speaking English all the way.)

As obvious as this may sound,
"Sit here," said he, "the sun comes round
So warm yourself as I do every day."

He built a house in Mexico
And knows exactly where to go
To build at half the cost to you and me.

He has a little Spaniel pet
Her temperament and manners set
To fit as dear a precious bitch as she.

He zip-lined Hong Kong's hoary heights
And gazed as Mumbai's brilliant lights
Fell soft on India's dingy western coast.

He witnessed women lifting hods
Arise five floors on stairs of rods
Feet bare, not touching rail nor steady post.

Some fell and died but no one cared,
For each some rupees had been spared,
And it seemed right and true just as he said it.

Humans and Other Animals

He told us tales with such conviction
No one dared to call them fiction,
Not one of them did any choose to edit.

Fantastic tales of daring told
Made each listener's blood run cold
As from his velvet sofa throne he spoke.

Four hundred pounds and legs so fat
One wondered how he even sat
Or zip-lined Asian skylines, what a joke!

We drank his wine—among the rarest—
But dusk fell on the Bay Banderas
As dregs befouled each listener's cloudy glass.

The smartest in the room was he,
Not one of us could fail to see,
And yet to us his righteous wine fell crass.

Our chance to speak was opportune,
Before arose the tropic moon,
Yet past it flew and in that hour
The smartest man had lost his power.

*Traveling central Mexico,
February 2012*

Squirrels and Thanksgiving

From my sunroom window
what do I see,
a squirrel or two
playing in a tree?

In November don't you think
they'd be gathering,
harvesting the pumpkin seeds
I've left for them
on the sunroom step?

But no, they chase,
they race and
take glee in a squirrel family's play.
They dart and jump
from trunk to branch to stump,
flip and fluff
their feather tails,
twist, turn, then confront
another furry face
on the back side
where I cannot see.

Humans and Other Animals

How assured are they;
faster and faster,
master of tree,
sky, and cloud;
no fear to fall, or fail to feed,
their nests full,
free of want and worry
of falling or freezing
in a frigid northern winter to come.

O were I so.

He ambles to the step
and takes a seed
and I another sip
from my coffee cup.

No worry
what the winter's to bring,
my furry friend;
I'll see you in the spring.

November 25, 2010

Stoning Dogs

Small brown boy
stands off the edge
of the path.

He bends to pick up
two stones
as big
as his tiny hands
will hold.

Why is he trembling?
What does he fear?

"*Se muerden?*" he asks –
(Do they bite?)
A dozen or so
small spotted dogs
raise a howl
of taunts, barks and yelps –
from pups pacing
the path, to the elders—

Humans and Other Animals

all related no doubt –
lazily witnessing,
watching, yipping
a warning.

They guard a corner
where a dry arroyo
adjoins two crosswise footpaths,
just where the craggy land rises
to meet the edge of the *pueblito*
On one side
and the *campo*
on the other.

How will he pass,
this terrified child
of six or seven years?
Is he going home?
To school?
Or to his *abuelita's*
for breakfast?

His fists are closed,
His fingers grasping
his defensive missile-rocks
so tightly that his knuckles
are nearly white.

Many's the time I've seen
Mexican boys stone dogs
—not out of meanness,
I suppose;
it's a cultural clang
I'm unfit to understand—
like the time
the son of Chiquita,
the neighbors' maid,
stoned our pet
Dobie Diana,
as she stood defenseless
behind our iron gates.

This time is different.
I know it at a glance.

The boy—I never
learned his name –
believes he must
defend himself
from a threat
very immediate;
though in truth
there is no threat
at all.

Humans and Other Animals

"*¿Se muerden?*" he repeats,
("Do they bite?")
as if I know this pack of dogs,
which I had just passed
coming from the country
leg of my morning walk.

"*No. No es necesario*", I say,
("It isn't necessary")
holding out my many-times-larger hand;
I open it and invite
him to drop the stones.

He looks up at me
from the dry creek-bed,
his owlish face twisted,
his chin trembling,
his sweet brown eyes darting
past me
to the dogs
                        beyond.

"*No muerden?*"
he repeats;
"*No; nada va pasar,*"
(Nothing's going to happen)

I answer,
extending my now-open
hand to him.

He drops the stones,
and climbs up the creek-bed
toward me,
accepting my hand.

"¿A donde vas?"
(Which way are you going?),
I ask as we come
to the well-guarded corner,
hounds clamoring
all about us.

Together we walk,
a strange sight perhaps –
tall *gringo*, tiny *muchacho*.

"*Es su trabajo de ellos,
a ladrar*" –
("It's their job to bark"),
I explain.
His gaze is fixed
over his shoulder
at the dogs.

Humans and Other Animals

Four more steps
up the rising path, and
the boy pulls his hand
from mine and moves
haltingly ahead,
more confidently now,
out of fear's way;
I guard his rear
from his imagined threat.

The boy turns back
toward me, escaping fear
with each step,
and says, "*Gracias.*"
I smile and wave him
on his way.

The incident
burns itself
into my memory
as I seek clarity,
about the boy,
me, the dogs—
all earth brothers,
yet each day
differently
    arrayed.

Aren't we all,
in our own way,
seeking peace,
fear-free lives,
elimination
of perceived threats?

In Costa Rica,
They disbanded
their armed forces
decades ago —
dropping the stones
in their hands
into the dry
creek-bed —
and the imagined
aggressors never came.

Dogs still bark
at their corners,
warning little boys
not to harm them
or invade
their space;
boys still
pick up stones.

And yet, we walk by
in peace.

February 24, 2013,
La Cruz de Huanacaxtle, Nayarit, Mexico

Tepid Revenge

Old hurts recalled reflect, arouse the pain
Of vicious slander, slur or hurtful slight;
Unwise it is to empower them again,
More than otherwise one might.

But temper rages so against it,
Though judgment counsel passion's cool surcease—
To placid turning-cheek can one submit—
Pardon the injured earned release.

Hate hurts the hater and avenges
Not at all the shiv the stabber thrust,
Though undeserving heart in pain yet twinges,
In hot and earnest yearning for blood's lust.

But "Kill 'em with kindness"; "Turn a frown upside down";
"Love thine enemy"; "Be a clown";
"Open up your heart and let the sun shine in."

Humans and Other Animals

Do these maxims may make you howl with laughter?
Maybe they're a step upon the path;
A fairy or a king lives happ'ly ever after,
(Once they've satisfied their raging wrath.)

The Flock

In the snow, a blizzard's fall of yesterday,
Forms what shape in the ravine, a vulture?
All black, though too big for a Crow, I say;
And suddenly it moves to make me ponder:

Wild turkey? Can it be, so isolated?
Where's the flock? (For turkeys never go alone.)
I scrutinize their pilgrimage, distracted;
They return, toward dangers unforeknown.

My work stalls now—as tallies press my weary mind;
A raven-shape outside my window pane
Is followed now by others out of line,
First one, then two, then six, as it begins to rain.

All mystery this dreary flock now satisfies,
Their rotund torsos, crooked beaks and broad dark wings
No longer can obscure their turkey lives;
I wonder too what sustenance a snowscape brings.

Humans and Other Animals

They pick a path from slope to creek-bed valley,
Treading snow, depart the pale of autumn cover.
Disorder in their ranks, they walk on heedlessly,
Trusting that their tom is not a rover.

The mindless flock rambles, then it slows
As predators—coyotes, foxes, wildcats—
Await them, hid beneath December snows,
Hunters also in their native habitats.

Do we, as they, trail listless, without aim,
Seeking, heedless, ignorant reprieve—
Yielding power without counter-claim,
Acolytes not risking disbelief?

November 28, 2015

(Under) The Porch

We always knowed that rats and cats and old
Dried-out boards with nails sticking out of 'em
was down there underneath the front porch.

Under the porch was somewhere you never
wanted yourself to go, 'less of course
you wanted to hide real bad and was willin'
to breathe some fine ol' dust and cat poop dirt
and maybe even sit on a nail to prove it.

The ground was all bumpy with rat-holes and rat crap;
there weren't much light down there 'cept where the boards
was broke, and the space where we crawled between
the loose ones and then put 'em back together.

Hidin' there was fun but not just
for Hide-and- Seek. Goin' behind a tree
or standin' on a porch behind a post
was good enough a hidin' place for that.

Beneath the porch was for some serious hidin'.

Humans and Other Animals

Sometimes I'd listen to ol' Mr. Russell hollerin'
at Mrs. Russell from down there—
stuff like bitch and slut and how she wanted
anythin' in pants, and the mailman would
go in and stay a while when Mr. Russell
was at work at the factory
till three in the afternoon.

Once we caught Little Joey down there and said
he took our plastic car and throwed it into
the pipe that stuck outta the wall of the house down there.
It weren't so, but we all hadta promise it was true.
We kept him there till it scared his mom so bad
she gived us a quarter to buy a new one.
And after that we still let Joey play with us,
but only not with the new plastic car.

When I was there I'd hear my sister Pat
talkin' and gigglin' and gossipin' with her girlfriends
from under there after school was out.
In the spring the teen-age girls took off their uniforms
as soon as they got home from school.

They tied their white blouses and t-shirts in front,
and wore tight jeans to show off for the boys.
And then the talkin'd stop and the girls'd walk
away and make room for Dad, comin' home from the bar;
I could tell who it was from the clump-scrape-bump and then
swearin' and two big ka-BUMPS when he fell,
grabbin' at the railing but it broke.
Dad was drunk and he falled on his hands and knees
before he could make it to the top of the stairs.
"What's wrong with your dad?" the girls asked Pat.
She said, "Nothin'," kinda quiet.

'Nuther time I memember Ricky
from down the street come by with a jump rope
in his hand when I was down under the porch.
He had long dark hair, and was always alone.
Ricky called to the girls, "Hey wanna jump rope?"
' n' they said yeah, 'n' next thing there's Ricky
singin' "Down in the Valley where the Green Grass Grows"
along with the best of 'em, and the boys comin' by
callin' him a sissy fur playin' with the girls, and Ricky—
taller but skinnier and paler than the guys—sayin'
"I got nails like a cat and I can scratch
yer eyes out, and I can tear you to shreds too;"
n' they seemed to believe him, 'cause they left him alone.
But Ricky was never sure what'd happen next time.

Humans and Other Animals

There was one time an older kid wanted to come
under the porch. Jimmy was his name and he was
twelve. He came onto our block one summer. He had
somethin' he wanted to show us, but he hadta
do it in secret; so me and Margaret and Ronnie
and Roberta let Jimmy come under the porch and Jimmy
said he hadta pee and stood up as much
as he could under there and pulled his wiener out.
It was dark—but not so dark we couldn't
see it; he didn't try to pee on us
but he stood close enough so's he might of.
It was big and pink and nothin' like
the ones I seen at school in the boys'-room
or in the shower-room at the rec center.

When he was done peein' Jimmy done somethin' to it,
shook it hard, 'n then it stood up
and Jimmy was shakin' hisself.
He made some noises in his throat,
and me and Margaret and Ronnie and Roberta just sat
and watched, but Jimmy giggled and then he laughed
real loud.

After that, I hadta go back to school,
and didn't have no time fur goin' down
under the porch no more. Mostly I don't
think 'bout it unless I think 'bout Jimmy
and then I wonder if Jimmy'll ever come back.

April 17, 1998

The Doing of a Thing

The doing of a thing and seeing it done
Are ways of work a worker uses,
But the finishing of it is far better won
When the joy of the work is the joy it produces.

June 10, 2016

The Glass

I looked into the glass today
And saw the Face of Death.
It peered intently at me,
I could nearly see its breath.

Why it so suddenly appeared
I'm not sure I can say.
It blinked, twisted, and weirdly smirked
As if it knew the day,

The hour, the minute, the second when
My mortal life would end.
It gave a wicked, rancid smile,
Snickered and with a grin

It pursed its lips to form a phrase
I read as "You shall perish."
I begged it: "Speak your secret,
Or now seize all I cherish."

Humans and Other Animals

It bore a startling likeness
To my own countenance;
It seemed to draw a laugh from death,
Amused I could not mount defense.

"If you can speak I beg you now
Reveal the date of your intention."
It rolled its bulging eyes to mock
My lack of comprehension.

In that flash of time I thought
I'd soon lose all that mattered;
It took a breath as if to speak;
With that the mirror shattered.

April 2016, Windsor, Ontario, Canada

To Marry?

So shall we marry?
Why now? we ask;
So daft a question
These decades past.

But if we shouldn't,
And missed this chance,
However would we
Obey life's urging: "Dance!"

> July 11, 2015, Douglas, Michigan, at the marriage
> of Mr. Ghislain (Gess) Malette and the author

Too Sensitive

Sensitive is the genius
Looking for a place to be –
A painter, dancer, a poet –
To fulfill his destiny.

Who among them has been told,
" Child, you're too sensitive,
Now go out and show it bold
To the world—not apprehensive."

"Show them you can play hard-ball;
Don't take no guff from bully-boys."
"If it hurts, you must stand tall,
Call each bluff, keep up your poise."

"We can beat it out of him;
That's how we'll know he's had enough;
Make of him a Tom or Jim;
Make a man of him—tough."

I once knew a boy like that,
His life an earthly dream from hell;
Never did he touch a bat,
Drew deep into a crusty shell;

All predators avoiding.
When no one saw or heard, he cried,
His Earth with other worlds colliding;
That night he hanged himself and died.

No more too sensitive was he,
Relieved at last no more to be.

Turkeys

A dozen turkeys passed me once,
An unmistaken sign of how
My soul no longer can be mine;
I'm captive of the country now.

The flock was so flawlessly formed—
I can't describe how prepossessed
The warmth that overcame me was
As they strutted from the forest.

On our land they hastened past me
From wood to clearing to brush again,
In urgency and symmetry,
Each movement measured, each tail a fan.

At first I thought them Canada Geese,
Their jackets contrasting dark and light,
But unlike other fowl they moved,
At steady pace and bolt upright.

On tips of horny claws they marched
Toward a ravine and then a creek,
To satisfy their eager-need,
To wet each bone-dry thirsty beak.

I wasn't meant to see them there,
For turkeys move in fear of man
And other hunters in the wood,
Else why is it that they ran

At such a lively, measured pace
Surprising, beguiling my startled gaze?
Each was a copy, evenly spaced—
Wrought by Nature to amaze—

To convey this city boy
To lands once old, now new,
To find a home he left behind
From sod-busting farmstead whence he grew—

From plainsman farmers once again.
I thank my settler Granddad "Paw"
On the fields of east Eye-Oh-Way,
As the avian drill team lifts each claw.

Humans and Other Animals

Oh how he worked with gnarled hands
To make a farmstead of his lands
Of geese and chickens, wheat, and corn,
Where turkeys, coyotes, and foxes were born.

There, giving-people traded favors;
No fences separated neighbors;
Turkeys that strayed from out the wood
Ran back as quickly as they could.

I'm back in the country; I'm home for good.

Ganges, Michigan, January 13, 2016

Two Burros

Two donkeys ran across the road, tethers
Trailing behind, and they raised hardly a brow
Because, well, donkeys (or burros,
As we call them here in Mexico)

Aren't exactly rare, you see, they run
From farms and fields nearby, where knots in ropes
They've cleverly chewed and untied,
Full of wild imaginings and high hopes.

They criss-crossed a file of buses,
Trucks and cars, just to test a dare
And folks with little time to watch them,
Glanced to see this comical pair.

But from where did they come? I speculated;
And where are they going? I wondered—
Maybe back home, if they can find it.
And on their hooves gaily thundered.

Humans and Other Animals

Out into a field of corn they flew,
Where yellow ears they'd always known of
Tempted them, but then they'd gallop,
Avoiding a bull guarding the grain they love.

Or maybe they're just kids out of school,
Making asses of themselves for fun,
Weaving through dangerous lanes of traffic,
Braying, bucking, on the run,

Grey eyes glazed like ladies who lunch—
(Before the shrimp—but after two cocktails),
Drunk on their freedom, evading all care,
Ears pointed backward, whipping their tails.

An hour later I passed them again,
The frolicsome couple smartly darting
Down a country sideroad lane,
Friends, ever-loyal, never parting.

Their jolly hour relishing, the gleeful pair
Lazed in the shade of a fruiting mango tree,
Gobbling fermented fruit, their favorite liquor,
Content as two burros ever could be.

February 21, 2015,
La Cruz de Huanacaxtle, Mexico

Weather Backcast

The weather on Wednesday was clousy;
Thursday was raining and dowsy;
Today is no better,
In fact it is wetter;
As a hair day,
It's partially frowzy.

December 20, 2013

What Exactly?

What Exactly Should it be,
Poetry?
In an age of gigabytes
Few delights
On hand-held screens amuse us humans
Except what means
"Where U IZ?;" "Watcha doin'?"
"Where ya goin'?"
These messages pass for a generation's
Communications?

But poety, be it rhymes
Or free-verse lines,
Arrives where other speech
Cannot reach.

How do we say love or a flower
With such power
As the poet can or could,
If she would?

Should she elect to vary the rhyme
Or change the rhythm set before,
Does love's sweet sentiment survive,
The flower flourish just the same?

Or will its love have fled the page,
The flower become disengaged,
Blossom lost its perfumed stamen?
No. Amen!

When I Was a Child

When I was a child
I thought they made
Peanut butter
From horse manure.

Perfectly logical
It was to me,
For they smelled
The same to my in-
Experienced nose.

Years since then
A little boy
came along
when I was planting
a honeysuckle
along the lot line
of our house.

As we prepared
To put manure
Into the hole
He poked a skinny
Finger through
The plastic bag
And into his mouth,
Before I could stop him.

But why should I?
He was merely
Testing the theory
Of the boy
I had been—
Wanting to taste
The source of the musky,
Mysterious
Aroma he'd smelled.

Could we adults learn
from these boys?

Humans and Other Animals

What do we think
The world holds
In store for us
Now that we know better
Than to eat
What merely
Smells good?

To measure
Life-mysteries against
The proofs of our senses,
Yes, that would give us
A more honest hint
Of what life's to bring—
A dollop of
Savory peanut butter,
Or a fingerfull
Of musty, stinking
Horse manure?

Yet I Am

A shadow of you hangs above me;
In that yearning blush of time
Presence I know as much as feel,
I am yours and you are mine.

You hover over me to lay a kiss:
And who is it you think you see,
When tender flesh meets mine
And your presence alters me?

Joys of passion yield to time apace,
While decades cede what years cannot divine;
Place transforms time, and so time place;
I see it in your face, and you in mine.

June 15, 2016

You Tried and Failed

You tried and failed to stop the rain,
And then to dry the melting snow
Befouling what became my grave;
Your failure sent their wet below.

Then bring the sun, I asked of you;
Its shine is needed in this place,
But light's heat wouldn't answer you,
To warm this chill upon my face.

A half-moon shone above my head,
But comfort from her didn't beam,
No solace came and so, instead,
The earth maintained its soggy scheme.

I asked you: Send a tree with roots
To pierce my darkened catafalque;
A tree you planted near my boots
To breach the ghastly earthen caulk.

In winter snows refused to cease;
In March the rains you could not stop,
But April's sun without surcease
Awoke the apple tree atop

My burrowed cell; from under
Its fingered roots crept, sucking, reaching,
Flaying flesh and bone asunder,
My rotting earthly corpus breaching.

In May you sent the rays to take
The gloom from out my moist retreat;
Your apple tree began to quake
Where pulp and bark and leafbud meet.

The summer's moon that failed before
Arose in streams so strong and bright
It focused on my cellar's door
To lift my coffin-top that night.

Unseen since last the moonrise showed
The sun shone down its blessed rays
And on the blossoms' pink-white glowed,
Fingers filigreed all ablaze.

Just then I reached from out my grave
To brush your cheek with apple bloom
And throve a life you couldn't save
Except through triumph over gloom.

February 14, 2014,
La Cruz de Huanacaxtle, Mexico

Acknowledgments

While writing a collection of poetry is primarily a solitary endeavor, the input and response of other writers to the material is invaluable before its publication.

I wish to offer special thanks to members of the La Cruz Writers' Group (LCWG) of Mexico, a writers' cooperative headed by Lynn Bradshaw, for their encouragement and support in publishing this book. Special appreciation is owed to Joylene Nowell Butler, Susan Appleyard, and Brenda C. Hill, all successful authors whose generous accolades grace the back cover of this book.

Author's Biography

Paul Edward Gainor was born in Detroit, Michigan in 1943 and earned a Bachelor of Arts Degree in Journalism and English from the University of Detroit. He was employed as a journalist at daily newspapers in Michigan, including The Detroit News, over 12 years. After a career in public relations with a New York-based agency for six years he led his own businesses in public relations, publishing, and marketing for a dozen years and from 1995 pursued a free-lance writing career until retiring in 1998. Besides writing poetry, Gainor volunteers with charities in Michigan and Mexico. Gainor and his spouse, Mr. Ghislain Malette, triangulate between homes in Fennville, Michigan, Windsor, Ontario, Canada and La Cruz de Huanacaxtle, Mexico.

Made in the USA
Lexington, KY
10 October 2017